Dear customer!

Thank you for purchasing our Halloween A

Life flies by at breakneck speed, like an arrow. We rush into this race, trying to catch up with every moment, every obligation, every goal. But in this endless whirlwind of tasks and worries, we often forget about the most important thing – ourselves.

Sometimes, in this race, we need to take time to stop. We need time for ourselves, to forget about worldly anxieties and simply be here and now. We search for ways to disconnect from this frenzied pace, to lose ourselves in the moment, enveloped in tranquility and harmony.

That's exactly why we're here – with our adult coloring pages. In this simple act of coloring, we find a way to express our creativity, to invest a piece of our soul into creating something beautiful. Here, there are no right or wrong answers, no judgments or deadlines. Here, there's only you and your imagination, dancing to the rhythm of colors and lines.

Coloring is not just a hobby; it's a way of relaxation and joy. It's a moment when we can allow ourselves to stop and look inside ourselves. It's a moment of truth, when we can find inner peace and harmony.

Looking for a creative and relaxing community? Join our coloring group on social media

ARTINK
PUBLISHING

Dear buyer!

Hope you're having fun with your new coloring book! If you've reached the end, I'm assuming you enjoyed it.

I wanted to chat with you about something important – your thoughts. The idea of asking for reviews didn't hit me right away. But as I thought more about it, I realized that happy customers often don't leave reviews, while those who didn't vibe with the book might be more vocal.

I'm committed to ensuring my coloring books are fairly evaluated, and your feedback is essential to achieving that.

To leave a review, simply scan the QR code below with your smartphone camera. It will take you directly to the Amazon review page for the coloring book you purchased.

Best regards,
Artink Publishing Team.

Made in the USA
Columbia, SC
21 September 2024